ALMOST TAKEN

THE STORY OF HOW I

ALMOST BECAME A STATISTIC

TANYA ROGERS

ISBN: **1535037008**
ISBN-13: **978-1535037006**

DEDICATION

To my parents David and Elsa Rogers for teaching me how to be prepared
when a situation like this comes up and giving me the support I need.

.

CONTENTS

ACKNOWLEDGMENTS

I wish to personally thank the following people for their contributions to my inspiration and knowledge and other help in creating this book:

My father, David Rogers, who encouraged me to tell my story and who helped me write and publish my book.

My mother, Elsa Rogers, who made sure I knew what to do if a situation like this ever happened to me and gave me the inspiration to tell my story to others so that they can learn from it.

My brother, Ethan Rogers, who is always supportive of the things I want to do.

I also wish to thank two people who I have not met in person but have always provided me and my family with the inspiration to do more, to write a book, to make more sales and to create a better life.

Grant Cardone and Caleb Maddix

CHAPTER 1
A MORNING LIKE ANY OTHER

It was finally here, summer vacation! This is the day I have been waiting for since last September. Don't get me wrong, I like school, in fact, I voluntarily enrolled in summer school just so I can skip a level in math for my 8th grade year. My dad was able to take a few vacation days so we could start out our summer vacation right, our annual trip to the Adventure Dome at Circus Circus in Las Vegas. So this is a day before my Vegas vacation! YES!

I was the first person awake in my house and I jumped out of the bed, quickly showered and got dressed. My plan for today was to go with my family and walk a couple laps around the park followed up by selling some chocolates to give myself some spending cash in Las Vegas. I woke my dad up at 8:15am, "PA! It's 8:15, time to wake up!" I know he gets up every day at 5am for work and this was his first time being able to sleep in, but this wasn't the day to do that. We had a full day planned out. Besides, he's always the one who tells me not to sleep in too late.

So my dad gets up and about 15 minutes later we get a phone call from a family friend (who was like a grandpa to us) saying that he was sick and asked if we could bring him some food and medicine. So of course we had to help. So now my mom and dad come up with a new plan for the morning. My mom and brother were going to bring the food and medicine while my dad drive's me to the park to sell some chocolates and then returns home to finish getting ready.

1

So we ate a quick breakfast and off my dad and I went. We got to our local park and got out of the car. My dad and I talked about the weather for a minute because it was very gloomy. The sky was overcast and had so much moisture in the air that it was sprinkling.

He tells me to be safe and then realizes that he did not have a cell phone to give me. Normally my mom is with me when I sell at the park or a store and she will usually shadow me and my brother to make sure we are safe. My dad was uncomfortable leaving me at the park with no way to call and not having my mom with me. But hey, I'm 12. At 12 years old my dad was riding his bicycle from Mission Viejo to San Juan Capistrano by himself.

So he told me to keep my eyes open and alert and to watch for him or my mom to come back to pick me up. I agreed with him and I started to make my rounds with the people who were nearest to me. I would go up to groups of people or individuals and would make my sales of these delicious chocolates. He went ahead and watched me for a few more minutes before he felt comfortable enough to leave. As I saw him pull away, I continued to make my rounds.

CHAPTER 2
I'M THE PREY AND HE'S THE HUNTER

So my time at the park seemed to be like a normal day. It was a little slower than usual due to the overcast weather, but there were still a good amount people there. So I started my time at the south end of the park. I hit the picnic tables first, but was not successful, not a single sale. I made way towards the north end of the park hitting the old playground next. Yes, I made a sale this time. Well, sort of, I got a one dollar donation. But hey, it's still income!

Now it was time to keep moving. I made my way north, passing through the middle of the park where the elderly people like to play cards. I hit up each table attempting to make my sales and I managed to get two more sales. Alright, that's great, I'm on my way to making some money today.

Now I am approaching the north side of the park, the "new park". I went to the area where people play baseball games, but no luck. Then I went to the playground and there was one family, but they politely declined. I needed a restroom break so I made my way towards the restroom. When I came out, he was there "tying his shoes." At first I thought he was just a man who was tying his shoes, but as soon as I walked forward he suddenly stopped and began following me.

At first, little did I realize who this person was? This was the man who would forever change the way I see things. This is the person that put more fear in my life than even the scariest movie character.

Luckily I have been prepared for this situation. Three weeks ago, my mom and dad were at the DMV and saw some missing child reports. My mom took note of the fact that they were in the past 30 days and were from the local community. This really got my mom thinking of how it's been a while since she's talked to me about something like this. As soon as she picked me up from school that day she was telling me about what she had seen. She told me about these missing children and the fact that they were all about my age.

That night when we got home, she had my dad immediately try to find the movie Taken starring Liam Neeson and Maggie Grace. My dad searched through the garage but was unable to find it. So she had him rent it online.

My mom and I sat on the sofa and began watching it. Throughout the movie, my mom would point out things for me to look for when I'm out on the street. She pointed out how kidnappers would find their victims by watching the crowds of people passing by. Most of the time they would look for a particular type of person. Once they found their victim, they would try to get themselves into a situation where they can make their move.

Some other things that she pointed out was when they came to kidnap the girls and Maggie Grace's character was on the phone with her dad. He coached her on what was about to happen and told her what things to look for about the kidnappers. He told her to say out loud, so that he can hear about any scars, facial marks or hair, height, weight, tattoos, hair color, clothing, skin color, and anything else that looks different.

So once the movie was finished my mom recapped with me all the different things I should be looking for. My mom had a genuine concern about the things that can happen in this world and she wanted to make sure I was prepared. She also knew she couldn't keep me in this bubble where I was protected from anything dangerous. In order to live your life, you have to take risks.

So now with this preparation came the moment where I had to execute on it.

As I walked away from the restroom, I acted calm and pretended not to notice that someone was following me. But I could feel that he had to be right behind me. I haven't looked back yet, but I could just feel it. I was starting to get really scared. The thought of this person following me was giving me a tingling sensation all over. I have never had this feeling before, I was starting to have a feeling of helplessness. But I tried not to show it.

As I walked across the park towards the main boulevard I could hear him making mumbling sounds and weird noises. As I approached the street I noticed that the noises had stopped. I turned my head and saw him walking to the parking lot and getting into a car. This felt like a moment from a movie where I looked back there was intensity in the air. I was looking back at him again in what can see is actually a truck, he looked straight at me as I was passing through the crosswalk.

During this time he started his truck and I heard the roar of the engine and then seconds later a red pickup zoomed past me and stopped a block in front of where I was. I could not see the person inside, but I knew that it was him.

When the truck passed, I saw something large in the back, but I couldn't tell exactly what it was. I continued walking with as much confidence as possible. When I came to where the truck had parked I glanced inside of it out of the corner of my eye, it was him!

I continued to walk and he followed. I traveled several blocks at this point and he stayed right behind me, driving in his truck at the same speed as I was walking. This went on for several blocks until I was stopped by some Jehovah Witnesses walking down the street. At this point he accelerated again, he blew past a red light and stopped at a bus stop a block ahead. When I excused myself from the Jehovah's and the light turned green I crossed the street.

As I crossed the street I looked around and started to think about what I should do next. In the time so far I have been lucky that there have been plenty of people around and a lot of businesses, but do I want to push that luck and keep going? No way! I'm not an idiot and I'm not going to keep letting this guy follow me.

I was at a major intersection with grocery stores, pharmacies, restaurants and more. This was a very busy location with lots of people around. He was still at the bus stop at the end of the block so I had to decide which place would be better to hide from him. I figured that he may think I went into the grocery store since there's more people there so I decided the safest place right now is a restaurant, which was also the closest to where I currently was. I went into the restaurant I explained to the cashier what had happened and I asked her if I could use the phone. I had to think about who to call first. So I called my dad, but he didn't answer. I immediately tried my mom, but she wasn't answering either. So, my only option was the house phone. I called and.........

CHAPTER 3
TO THE RESCUE (DAD'S PERSPECTIVE)

I was back home starting to get ready for the day. I had cleaned up outside and got my stuff together to take a shower when my phone rang. I came to the living room and saw a number I did not recognize, I hesitated for a moment and thought it may be a telemarketer and I didn't really feel like dealing with that. But then I thought "oh wait! It could be Tanya using someone's phone from the park" maybe she needed something. So I pressed to answer the call, but too late, it just stopped ringing.

So I called the number back to find out who it was and it rang busy. "Oh, maybe she is leaving a voicemail" I thought.

So a minute later the house phone rang and it was the same number so I answered it quickly this time. This was it, this was the sound that no parent wants to hear, the tone of the voice, the trembling and shakiness of it, immediately raising my concern to the highest level it could be at.

"Pa" the voice said with worry and fear.

"Tanya, what happened!?" I immediately replied.

At this moment during the brief second between us speaking the words out loud, I had flashes of someone robbing her at the park when they saw her selling and getting money.

After what felt like an eternity, she spoke again, "Pa, someone is following me."

And that did it, the one thing that could raise my concern beyond where it already was. "Tanya where are you, what happened!?" I said without hesitation.

"I am at the restaurant by the grocery store..." she continued to speak, but I can't recall her exact words at this point.

I had flashes of Liam Neeson's character in the movie Taken when he was talking to his daughter on the phone as she was being kidnapped. I quickly confirmed where she was at that moment and told her to stay right there and I would be there to get her.

My heart now racing like I had been shot with adrenaline a thousand times. I dropped the phone to the floor, grabbed my keys, cell phone, and wallet in one swift move and ran out the front door to my truck.

It was like time had slowed down around me. Everything seemed so clear as I ran to my truck and opened the door and flew up into the driver's seat. Keys in the ignition and starting the vehicle immediately followed by the gear shift going into reverse. Pedal slammed to the floor my truck tires spun out of control until the rubber gripped the road. This is the fastest I had ever driven in my driveway.

Stopping just short of the sidewalk to look for any pedestrians walking by, good no one! Pulled back to the edge of the street to look for oncoming cars, good clear! Pedal once again slamming to the floor and wheels spinning out of control as I started moving backwards.

In the street now and already looking ahead two streetlights I needed to figure out which way I would go. I see that the light just turned red and already had several cars waiting in the turn lane that I needed, no good! As I'm accelerating down the road I look for the first and only side street before the main boulevard. I quickly look around for any pedestrians and it's clear.

I turn the corner while looking ahead seeing that the street is empty and start to accelerate during my turn. As I come to the cross streets

I am looking very carefully for other cars, kids, and anything else that could be in my way. I know that I need to be there faster than fast, but I also know that I cannot endanger someone else's life in the process and I must use caution driving down these small side streets. So I continue to scan around looking for potential hazards and see none. I slam the gas pedal to the floor once again and accelerate very quickly through the stop sign.

At the next corner coming up I have to make a decision on which way I want to go. I can make a right at the corner and head to the boulevard or I can continue straight and pass through several intersections like the last ones I did. Well, I decided to make the right, it's the safest choice. I scan around like I did at the previous corner and see it is clear so I accelerate during my turn again and continue to pick up speed as I drive down the road. Flying over speed bumps heading towards my next decision, the red light that's at the corner in front of me. I know this corner is too dangerous for me to just fly through like I did the previous few times so I come to a stop right before the light. Luck is with me, as soon as I stop the light turns green.

You can imagine what I did next, I let the pedal hit the floor as I made my left turn. Now on the main boulevard I had to increase my scanning of the road. I had many vehicles around me, increased number of pedestrians and the police to worry about. Well, my daughter's safety outweighed my concern about the police, besides, I figured I was going to need their help pretty soon anyway.

I continued to drive very aggressively and heavy footed. This caused most of the vehicles in front of me to move out of my way. The ones that didn't move I quickly zoomed around and probably did so before they even noticed what was going on. Luck was still with me. Most likely due to the overcast weather the streets were not as busy as they normally would be. This drive can take 10 minutes when there is full traffic on the street. Here I am at one to two minutes in and I am almost there.

Now here I am, one street light away, but still a couple blocks and stuck at a red light. First in my lane my eyes are in front of me waiting for the light to change. At this point there are too many cars crossing the road and I have to wait this eternity for the light to change and it finally does. I take this 7,000 pound beast from 0-60 in what feels like a heartbeat. I am finally almost there. This whole time just hoping and praying that she is safe and there ready for me to pick her up.

I continue down the road till I'm about to enter the parking lot of the shopping center she's at. I quickly look down the street at the oncoming cars and they are still a block away. I check for pedestrians to see if anyone is going to be crossing the road or driveway and there is no one around. So I make my final acceleration going into the parking lot and taking the first right headed straight toward the restaurant she called from.

I'm still looking around for any hazards and start looking for her as well but I don't see anything. So I come to a screeching halt into two parking spaces in front of the restaurant. I throw it in park and remove my keys just as swiftly as I put them in earlier.

I jump out my truck and run to the front of the restaurant where there's two employees staring at me from behind the counter. I again quickly glance around and do not see Tanya anywhere, not even in the restaurant.

My heart racing even faster than before, I'm now getting even more worried. I quickly think to myself that maybe she is behind the counter in the restaurant since she used their phone. So I race into the restaurant and as the door opens I say "I'm looking for my daughter, she…" then I look to the left and see Tanya sitting right there beside the counter.

OH THANK YOU GOD YOU'RE SAFE NOW! I think to myself.

"Let's get in the truck" I tell her with urgency.

We get into my truck and I immediately lock the doors. Now that I know she's safe and under my protection I ask her what happened.

CHAPTER 4
NOW THE HUNTER BECOMES THE PREY

Now that we are safe and I explained everything that happened to my dad it was time for us to decide what to do. My dad's first instinct was to take me home and away from all this. Who could disagree with this idea? But could we really just leave and let this guy get away with this and possibly do it to someone else. Of course we couldn't.

My dad started by asking what vehicle he was driving and where exactly was the last place I saw him. Well, during my time being followed and being able to see him several times I had committed certain details about him and his vehicle to memory. I immediately told my dad that he was driving a red Toyota Tacoma pickup and that it had some large object in the back of it. At this time I also had looked over at the bus stop that he originally was waiting at and saw that he was no longer there, so I let my dad know that as well.

We started driving in the parking lot and were looking around to see if he moved to another location. My dad headed towards the exit and then made a right turn going more into the parking lot. Just as we turned the corner my dad pointed across the parking lot at a red Toyota Tacoma with a large object in the back and asked me, "Tanya, is that the truck?"

"Yes, that's it" I replied.

My dad made a right turn in the first available lane, a couple lanes away from where the truck was parked. We pulled into a space and looked around, but did not see him anywhere around the truck or the sidewalk. So at this point my dad drove around the outside of the parking lot and pulled in right behind his truck.

He got out of our truck and locked the doors with his remote. He then casually walked pass the truck while looking for anybody who may be watching us. He did not see anyone so he came back around and pulled out his iPhone and started to take pictures of every angle around the truck. He got the sides of the truck, the front and rear ends, including the license plates and then he also took pictures of the inside of the truck as well.

Just as casually he walked back to our truck, unlocked it with his remote and got back in. He then started it, backed up and pulled away like nothing happened. As we proceeded back to the parking space across the lot again where we last were he told me that the guy had a large dog cage or animal carrier in the back of the truck.

"A dog cage?" I replied.

"Yes and large enough for a small person to fit in it" he said.

He asked me to give him the details of what the guy looked like.

"He was wearing a black Adidas sweater and black Climacool pants with orange stripes in the middle of each side. He had fluorescent orange Nike shoes with black sole and he was wearing a gray shirt that had different colored geometric shapes. He looked like he was Latino and had an almost bald haircut and in his 30's. It looked like he had a scar or mark on his forehead right in between his eyebrows." I told my dad.

The look of his face was enough to scare someone. His face would give someone the chills. But wouldn't you feel the same if it was you being followed?

We waited in the parking space for a few minutes looking around for something but nothing. Then it happens. My dad quickly asks me, "is that him?"

"Yes" I replied.

He was coming out of the grocery store carrying a bouquet of flowers. Were these flowers that he was going to use to try to tempt me to come near his vehicle? Does he have a wife at home that he bought these for? Is it for another person that perhaps he has locked up at home? I just don't know what's going on! But what I do know is that it was him and I was now safe with my dad.

My dad said as he saw this guy walk towards his truck he had several thoughts running through his mind at that time. He was debating on what course of action he should take. The first thought he had was to take his 7,000 pound truck and run him over. But that won't necessarily help the situation. Should he ram this guy's truck with our own truck? No, that could put me in jeopardy again. Well, now the guy had gotten into his truck and started it up and we had to make a decision. What will it be?

Well, he made what I think was the best decision. We decided to follow this guy. The guy started to head out of the parking lot using a different exit than where he came in. He got to the edge of the driveway and my dad started our truck and put us into drive. We let the guy pull out of the parking lot and into the street before we came to the driveway ourselves.

At this point my dad pulled out his phone, dialed 911 and put it on speaker.

"911 what's your emergency?" The operator said.

My dad continued to tell the 911 operator what had happened and that we were in pursuit of the suspect. The 911 operator lets us know that she was dispatching officers and wanted to stay on the line with us so we can keep her updated on our location.

Well the pursuit continued. The suspect made a right at the first side street he came to and proceeded to drive at a normal speed. He stopped at the next major street and made another right headed back to the boulevard. We stayed about 1-2 blocks behind the suspect so that he would not notice us following. When he got near the corner of the boulevard he surprised us by making an illegal left turn into the parking lot of a little Hispanic market. My dad continued past this location crossing the boulevard.

As soon as we crossed we made a quick left into the parking lot of a bank. We pulled through the rear of the lot and headed towards the exit of the lot on the boulevard side. My dad quickly parked in between some other cars near the exit and continued to watch the suspect. We gave the 911 operator the update that he was in the market and had not left yet. We waited for several minutes and then he finally came back out. We let the operator know that he was back and about to leave.

He now pulled out his parking place and headed towards the exit of the market. My dad not wasting anytime backed our truck out of the parking spot it was in and headed to the driveway. He quickly dashed out into the street and made a left turn in the direction we thought he was heading. At this point the suspect was still waiting to leave the parking lot he was in so we quickly pulled into a 7-11 parking lot across the street, but as we did this the suspect quickly pulled out of his parking lot and illegally crossed straight into the 7-11 parking lot himself. He literally passed just a couple feet from our truck, but luckily my dad's truck has tinted rear windows and he could not see me in the back seat (I think).

The suspect just pulled through the 7-11 parking lot and exited through the place where we came in at. So my dad pulled through as well and exited on the side the suspect entered from. We made two quick rights and were in pursuit again. We still let the suspect stay 1-2 blocks ahead of us because we did not want to spook him and cause him to run. We knew the police were close by and we've still been giving our updated locations. So we just needed to watch him long enough for the police to catch up to him.

So we continued down the boulevard passing the last location where he was still hunting me. We came to a corner a few blocks away from there and he made a right heading away from the main street and onto the side streets. We hoped that he didn't catch on to us following him and that he was going to try to make a getaway.

As we made the right turn 20-30 seconds later that did not appear to be the case. He was still driving casually and appeared to be headed somewhere or perhaps he was looking around for me hoping I lived in this area.

He made a left at the next corner and we followed. While giving the 911 operator our current location she got a call on the radio from the police officers in route that they were around the corner and would be with us in less than a minute. Oh man was that a relief to hear. Finally, this will all be coming to an end.

CHAPTER 5
POLICE ASSISTANCE

We were driving down the road, the suspect is two blocks in front of us and in our rear view mirror we see the police cruiser coming up behind us. We pull to the right to allow him to go past us and he zooms by. We are still in motion and pull back into the street right behind him. We allow some distance to come between us and the cruiser so that we can get a better view of what's about to happen.

The next thing you know the police officer kicked on his lights and siren and had the suspect pull over to the right. As he was pulling over the suspect a second police officer pulled up from a side street to assist the first officer.

They approached the vehicle and had the suspect get out of his vehicle with his hands up. They performed the usual search of the suspect and then they did the best part of all. They put him in handcuffs. He looked so surprised to be put into handcuffs.

Luckily, when the police pulled the suspect over they knew it was him because while we were in pursuit my dad had given me the phone to tell the 911 operator the exact description of the suspect. Just like I had told my dad when he asked me to tell him what the guy looked like I was able to tell the 911 operator. So there was no confusion about who this guy was.

We pulled around the corner of the side street where the police officers pulled over the suspect. My dad positioned our truck next to a tree so that the suspect would not be able to see me in the window. Even though the windows are tinted he did not want to take that chance. But he did position us just right that I was able to turn around and still get a good look at what was going on. Ah, to see this creep in handcuffs sitting on the curb felt so good.

While one officer stayed with the suspect the other officer came over to our vehicle. He spoke with my dad for a couple minutes outside of the truck and then he came and sat in the back seat with me. He asked me what happened. If the suspect did anything inappropriate. If he exposed any part of his body to me. If he attempted to make any contact with me or say anything directly to me. I let the officer know that he did not do any of those things.

So the officer let me and my dad know that because he did not do anything except stalk me that there is nothing to charge him with. If he had attempted anything else at all they would be able to do something about it. He did let us also know that they will check for any criminal record for this guy and if there is anything there they might be able to do something with that. He said in the worst case scenario that he and his partner would have a very serious conversation with the suspect and make sure he thinks twice before attempting anything like this again.

Once he finished talking with us he advised us to go ahead and go home so that the suspect would not see us there. My dad hopped back in the truck and we pulled away. So even though we left it was good to know the cops were getting it under control.

CHAPTER 6
IN SUMMARY

I look back at what happened and see I could have done some things differently. Like when I was walking from the park to the restaurant where I eventually stopped at, I could have stopped several times before that at busy stores or restaurants like a 7-11 for instance. Even though there were other places I could've stayed, most people in the community speak Spanish and it would've been harder for me to ask to use the phone or explain what was happening. But by traveling farther like I did I had given him more opportunity to take me. But in the end if I had done anything differently, I may have had a different and less desirable result.

Unfortunately the suspect did not get in any trouble that I am aware of. My parents have seen him again at the park since that time. However we now have a picture of the suspect on top of the photos that my dad took that day of his vehicle and license plate number. We also know where he hangs out at the park and the people he hangs out with. If anything should ever happen in the future we have information that can help.

I have done some research online and would like to share some of this information with you. I have gotten information from a couple different sources and you can find links to those websites in the bibliography at the end of this book.

Here are some key points and takeaways

- Even though this is a very scary situation there are things you need to do when you are in a situation like this.

- You need to be observant and alert. Pay attention to what is going on around you.

- Try to determine if someone is in fact following you by speeding up and slowing down to see if they copy your moves, or try crossing the street.

- Do not panic. You need to stay calm and alert at this point.

- Look for a safe place to stay. Look for busy stores or restaurants that you can go into.

- If you have a cell phone with you, call 911. Alert them to the situation and where you are currently at and heading. You can also announce out loud that you are calling the police as this may deter the suspect.

- If you are still being followed, you can always turn around and look directly at the suspect. This in some cases will deter the person from continuing to follow you. But do not stay in one place for too long.

- If the suspect is still continuing to follow, you can start to scream or yell to get other people's attention. The goal here is to get people to notice you and to deter the suspect from pursuing.

- You can run to get away, but make sure that you do not go anywhere that may cause you to get cornered or trapped.

Now there are also things you will want to look for while this is happening. You need to start making mental notes about the suspect to give information to the police, family members or other people.

- What clothes is the suspect wearing (Shirt, pants, jackets or sweaters, shoes, socks, hats, gloves)? What type and color, any logos or designs?

- What does the suspects face look like? Any scars or markings, facial hair, skin color, eye color, hair color, ears, anything that can help identify?

- What does the suspect's hair look like? Hair color, style or bald?

- What does the suspect's body look like? Approximate weight, height, skinny, medium or large, any marks or tattoos, do they look like a body builder or scrawny?

- Do they have any watches or jewelry?

- Are they driving a vehicle? What is the year, make and model? What color is the vehicle? Is it an SUV, car or truck? Does it have anything inside that stands out? What is the license plate number?

These are just some of the things that you can look for. Do some more research online and get more tips on what to do. Your safety is the number one priority.

Here are some statistics about child abduction

- Every 40 seconds a child becomes missing or abducted

- In 2001, 840,279 people (adults and children) were reported missing to the FBI's National Crime Information Center (NCIC). The FBI estimates that 85 to 90 percent of those (roughly 750,000 people or 2,000 per day) reported missing were children. The vast majority of these cases are resolved within hours.

- There are 3 types of kidnapping: kidnapping by a relative of the victim or "family kidnapping" (49 percent), kidnapping by an acquaintance of the victim or "acquaintance kidnapping" (27 percent), and kidnapping by a stranger to the victim or "stranger kidnapping" (24 percent).

- Only 1 out of 10,000 missing children reported to the local police is not found alive.

- In 80 percent of abductions by strangers, the first contact between the child and the abductor occurs within a quarter mile of the child's home.

- Most potential abductors grab their victims on the street or try to lure them into their vehicles.

- About 74 percent of the victims of nonfamily child abduction are girls.

- Acting quickly is critical. Seventy-four percent of abducted children who are ultimately murdered are dead within three hours of the abduction.

Now take these statistics as a guide. I don't know exactly how long ago this article was published but I see it as a way to open my eyes to the things that go on around me every day. Now remember that even though there are risks around us every day. We can't stop living our lives because of them. Risks are a part of life and we need to be prepared the best we can to not allow anything bad to happen to us. There are things I did that I believe helped me to not have been taken, but it could have been a different story if it were someone else.

Parents please make sure your children are prepared for something like this and that they can remember these things I have talked about. If you believe that you may have someone who is following you please report it to your local police department. This information may help prevent you or someone else from being taken or worse.

If you have a story or tips that you would like to share please contact me. You can e-mail me at Tanya@tanyarogers.com or visit my website www.tanyarogers.com

CHAPTER 7
FAMILY DISCUSSION WORKSHEET

I truly believe that the information that my mom and dad discussed with me helped keep me safe. This chapter is for you and your family to have a discussion about this subject. The pages have blank spaces so that you can write in them and answer the questions or make notes.

Do you think that Tanya was expecting something like this to happen to her that day? How do you think she thought her day would go?

Do you think that this can ever happen to you? Why or why not?

How often does a child go missing or is abducted?

Do you think any of them ever thought it would happen to them?

What are some places you think this can happen at?

What is the most common type of abduction?

- Stranger kidnapping
- Family kidnapping
- Acquaintance kidnapping?

Why do you think this is the most common type?

What are some ways you can reduce the chance of acquaintance kidnapping?

What are some ways you can reduce stranger kidnapping?

What are some ways you can reduce family kidnapping?

If you think you have someone following you, what should you do?

What are some details that you should remember about the potential kidnapper?

Who do you call if something like this happens to you?

If you are being followed, where should you go?

Make a plan with your family that if anyone ever gets lost or separated where should you meet?

Although not completely related to this subject, does your family have an emergency preparedness plan? What is that plan?

Why should you be alert to your surroundings?

Why is it important to remain calm?

What are your thoughts about this subject?

Why is it important to be prepared?

BIBLIOGRAPHY

Key points and takeaways:

Parts of this section are from an article provided by wikiHow, a wiki building the world's largest, highest quality how-to manual. Please edit this article and find author credits at wikiHow.com. Content on wikiHow can be shared under a Creative Commons License." http://www.wikihow.com/Avoid-an-Attack-if-You-Think-You%27re-Being-Followed

Statistics from Parents.com:

Bilich, Karin A. (n.d.) "Some important information about kidnappings in the U.S." Parents.com. Retrieved on June 18, 2016 from http://www.parents.com/kids/safety/stranger-safety/child-abduction-facts/

www.ingramcontent.com/pod-product-compliance
Lightning Source LLC
Chambersburg PA
CBHW061939280526
45787CB00004B/1652